Michael Anthony Mariani

Unfailing GRACE

How GOD'S Grace Transforms Broken lives

Published by Hemingway Publishers

Cover design by Hemingway Publishers

ISBN: Printed in the United States

Dedication

To my daughter, Chelsea—You are never far from my heart. No matter the distance, no matter the years, no matter the past—you have always been, and will always be, my daughter. I love you more than words can carry. There were seasons in my life where I fell short. Seasons where I lost my way. And I know those moments created space between us that was never meant to be there.

If I could go back, I would. If I could undo certain things, I would. But what I can do now… is stand in truth.

You have never been forgotten. You have never been unloved. Not for one moment.

This book is a reflection of the grace that changed my life—and my prayer is that same grace reaches you, restores what was broken, and brings us back together again.

I believe in that. And I will never stop believing in you.

With all my love,

Dad

To my Pops—

Thank you.

Thank you for never turning your back on me… even when I gave you every reason to. Thank you for standing by me when life got hard, when I was lost, when I was walking through storms of my own making. There were moments I didn't believe in myself… but you never stopped believing in me.

You saw something in me when I couldn't see it. You held the line when I was slipping. You stayed when it would have been easier to walk away. That kind of love changes a man. And I carry that with me.

Because of you, I kept going. Because of you, I didn't give up. Because of you, I'm still standing. I am who I am today—in part because you never quit on me. And I will never forget that.

With deep gratitude and love.

Your son,

Michael

Special Thanks

There are moments in life when everything feels dark… when you reach a place where you know you can't carry it on your own anymore. And in one of those moments, I cried out to God. Not with polished words. Not with strength. But from a place of real need. And He answered.

Melissa,

I don't believe for a second that it was a coincidence that you reached out to me. You were a stranger. Someone I didn't know. And yet, at exactly the right time—when I needed it most—you showed up. God used you in a way I will never forget. In a season where I was struggling, where things felt heavy and dark, you became a light. A voice of encouragement. A presence of kindness.

A reminder that I wasn't alone. You may not have seen the full weight of what that meant in the moment… but I did. And I still do. Because I know it wasn't random. It was God. I had cried out to Him… and He answered—by placing you in my path. Thank you for listening. Thank you for caring.

Thank you for being willing to reach out when you didn't have to. You were the catalyst that helped me move through one of the hardest times in my life. And I will always be grateful for that.

God sends people when we need them most. And for me… He sent you.

Table of Contents

Author Bio
Michael

Michael is an ordained minister, a devoted follower of Jesus Christ, and a man whose life stands as a testimony to the transforming power of God's grace. At 54 years old, his journey has been marked by both deep struggles and profound redemption—experiences that now fuel his passion to reach others with truth, hope, and the Gospel.

Having walked through seasons of personal hardship, including past addictions, broken relationships, and the weight of regret, Michael understands firsthand what it means to fall—and what it means to be lifted back up by the mercy of God. Rather than hiding his past, he uses it as a platform to reveal the reality of grace: *that no life is too far gone, and no failure is beyond God's reach.*

As a minister, Michael is committed to serving others through teaching, encouragement, and spiritual guidance. He is authorized to perform marriages, baptisms, and last rites, but more importantly, he seeks to lead people into a real and personal relationship with Jesus Christ. His approach is direct, honest, and rooted firmly in Scripture, with a desire to speak truth without compromise.

Michael's writing reflects his heart—to awaken those who are drifting, restore those who feel broken, and remind every reader that God's grace is not just a concept, but a life-changing reality. His message is clear: no matter where you've been, God is still calling—and it's not too late to answer.

Above all, Michael is a man who loves God, values truth, and longs to see lives changed by the same grace that changed his.

Michael is a writer, minister, and truth-seeker whose work is deeply rooted in faith, redemption, and the enduring pursuit of God's presence in everyday life. Drawing from personal trials, spiritual awakening, and a lifetime of reflection, his writing speaks to the broken-hearted, the searching, and those yearning for something deeper than surface-level belief. His voice carries the weight of lived experience—honest, unfiltered, and anchored in Biblical truth.

What sets Michael apart is not just what he writes, but how he writes. His style is deliberate and immersive, blending poetic cadence with theological depth. Each sentence is crafted with intention; every word is strategically placed, not merely to inform, but to resonate. His prose flows with a rhythmic, almost meditative quality—inviting readers to slow down, reflect, and absorb the message in its fullness. There is a distinct weight to his wording, where pauses, emphasis, and structure all serve a higher purpose: to deliver truth with clarity, beauty, and conviction.

Michael's writing does not rush. It lingers where it matters. It presses into the tension between human weakness and divine grace, often illuminating profound spiritual truths through simple yet piercing expressions. His unique sentence construction—layered, purposeful, and deeply expressive—creates an experience where the message unfolds with both power and elegance. Readers don't just read his words; they feel them.

At its core, his work is a ministry in written form—calling people back to Christ, back to truth, and back to the understanding that even in brokenness, there is purpose, and through God, there is always redemption.

Foreword

There are many books written about grace. But very few truly confront it. Because grace, when rightly understood, is not soft. It is not passive. And it is not something that allows a person to remain the same. Real grace challenges, exposes, humbles, and ultimately transforms.

That is exactly what you are about to encounter in this book.

Unfailing Grace: How God's Mercy Transforms Broken Lives is not written from a place of theory. It is written from the reality of a life that has wrestled, fallen, and been restored. That matters—because grace is not best understood in comfort, but in the moments when a person realizes they cannot save themselves.

In these pages, you will not find watered-down truth or empty encouragement. You will find Scripture presented with clarity, conviction, and urgency. You will be reminded that grace is not permission to continue in sin, but the power to come out of it. You will be confronted with the reality that while God's mercy is freely given, it must be received—and that moment of decision cannot be postponed forever. This book does not simply explain grace—it calls you to respond to it. Whether you are someone who has walked with God for years, someone who feels distant and unsure, or someone who has never fully surrendered your life to Christ, this message meets you where you are. But it will not leave you there.

You will be challenged.

You will be convicted.

And if you allow it, you will be *changed.*

The message within these pages is simple, but it is not easy:

God's grace is real.

It is available.

And it is enough.

But it requires surrender.

As you read, do not rush. Let the words settle. Let the Scriptures speak. And most importantly, be honest with yourself about where you stand with God. Because by the time you reach the end of this book, you will not just have learned about grace—you will have been given the opportunity to receive it. And that is a moment that should never be taken lightly.

Introduction

A World Desperate for Grace

There has never been a time in human history when people did not need the grace of God. Every generation faces brokenness, failure, sin, and regret. But behind every wounded life stands a truth that many struggle to believe: God has not abandoned humanity. Grace is the reason we are still here.

Many people think grace is simply kindness from God, but Scripture reveals something much deeper. Grace is God reaching down to people who cannot save themselves. It is love given freely to those who do not deserve it. This is the story of the Bible.

From Genesis to Revelation, God continually extends grace to flawed and struggling people. Kings who failed. Prophets who ran. Disciples who doubted. Even those who persecuted the church. Yet God did not discard them. Instead, He transformed them.

This book explores a powerful truth that many believers know in theory but struggle to live in reality: God's grace is greater than our worst failures. And when we truly understand grace, it changes everything. It changes how we see God. It changes how we see ourselves. And it changes how we live.

Chapter 1
What Is Grace?

Grace is one of the most talked-about words in Christianity. And yet, for something so central, it is one of the most misunderstood. People use the word "grace" casually. They say it when they talk about forgiveness. They mention it when they speak about blessings. Some even reduce it to nothing more than God being "nice" or "kind." But grace is not softness. Grace is not weakness. And grace is not God lowering His standard. Grace is God making a way where there was no way.

Grace Defined by Scripture

The clearest definition of grace is found in the Word of God:

"For by grace are ye saved through faith; and that not of yourselves: it is the gift of God: Not of works, lest any man should boast."

— Ephesians 2:8–9

That verse cuts straight through human pride. It tells us something we don't naturally want to accept: You cannot earn salvation. Not by effort. Not by discipline. Not by being "a good person." Grace is a gift. And a gift, by definition, is not something you earn.

Why Grace Offends Human Pride

Here's the truth most people struggle with:

We want to deserve what we receive. We want to feel like we earned it. Like we worked for it. Like we proved ourselves worthy. That's how the world operates. But God's Kingdom does not run on human effort. It runs on grace. And that's why grace offends pride.

Because grace says: You are not as good as you think you are. And you are not capable of saving yourself.

That's hard for people to accept. But until you accept that truth, you cannot truly receive grace.

Grace Is Not a License to Sin

Now this is where many people get it wrong. They hear that grace is free—and they assume it means there are no consequences.

They think:

"I can live how I want… God will forgive me."

"I'm under grace, so it doesn't matter."

That thinking is dangerous. The Apostle Paul addressed this directly:

"What shall we say then? Shall we continue in sin, that grace may abound? God forbid."

— Romans 6:1–2

That's not a suggestion. That's a correction. Grace is not permission to stay in sin.

It is the power to come out of it.

Grace Meets You Where You Are—But Doesn't Leave You There

Here's the balance you need to understand:

Grace will meet you in your brokenness. But it will not leave you in it. God doesn't say: "Fix yourself, then come to Me." He says, "Come to Me, and I will change you."

That's the difference. Grace is not God ignoring your sin. Grace is God dealing with your sin through Jesus Christ.

Grace Was Paid For

A lot of people talk about grace as if it were free. But it wasn't free. It cost everything.

"But God commendeth his love toward us, in that, while we were yet sinners, Christ died for us."

— Romans 5:8

Jesus paid for grace with His life. The cross was not symbolic.

It was a substitution. He took the punishment that belonged to you. He carried the weight you deserved. And because of that, grace became available.

Grace and Truth Go Together

There's another mistake people make; they try to separate grace from truth. They want grace without conviction. They want forgiveness without accountability. But Scripture makes it clear.

"And the Word was made flesh, and dwelt among us... full of grace and truth."

—John 1:14

Not grace alone. Not truth alone. Both.

Truth exposes the problem. Grace provides the solution. If you remove truth, grace becomes meaningless. If you remove grace, truth becomes crushing.

God gives both.

What Grace Really Means for You

Grace means—you don't have to pretend anymore. You don't have to carry guilt forever. You don't have to stay stuck in the same cycle. But it also means—you can't stay the same. Because when grace truly takes hold of your life, something changes. Not overnight. Not perfectly. But undeniably. Your desires shift. Your heart softens. Your direction changes.

A Hard Question

Let me ask you something, honestly.

Have you received grace…or have you just heard about it? Because there's a difference.

You can know the verses. You can agree with the message. You can sit in church for years. And still never surrender.

Grace is not something you admire; it's something you accept.

The First Step

If you want to understand grace fully, it starts here: Humility and acknowledging.

"I can't save myself."

"I need God."

"I need forgiveness."

That's where grace begins. And once it begins… it will start changing everything.

Chapter 2
Grace From the Beginning

A lot of people think grace is a New Testament idea. They believe grace showed up when Jesus came. But that's not true. Grace has been part of God's nature from the very beginning. If you miss that, you miss the full picture of who God is.

The First Failure—and the First Act of Grace

Go back to the beginning. Before sin. Before shame. Before separation. Adam and Eve walked with God in perfect fellowship. There was no guilt. No fear. No distance. And then came the fall.

They disobeyed God, not by accident, not by ignorance, but by choice. And in that moment, everything changed. Sin entered. Shame followed. And separation began.

"And the eyes of them both were opened, and they knew that they were naked..."

— Genesis 3:7

For the first time, humanity felt exposed. And what did they do? They hid.

Human Nature Hasn't Changed

That reaction is still the same today. When people sin, they don't run to God. They run from Him. They hide. Behind excuses. Behind distractions. Behind pride.

Adam said: "I heard thy voice in the garden, and I was afraid... and I hid myself."

— Genesis 3:10

Fear replaced fellowship. That's what sin does.

God Came Looking Anyway

Now this is where grace shows up. God didn't walk away. He didn't abandon them. He came looking.

"And the Lord God called unto Adam, and said unto him, Where art thou?"

— Genesis 3:9

Understand this: God knew where Adam was. That question wasn't for information. It was an invitation. Grace always reaches first. Even when you're hiding. Even when you've failed. Even when you know you're wrong. God still calls.

Judgment Was Real—But So Was Mercy

Let's not soften this. There were consequences. Sin always carries consequences. Adam and Eve were removed from the garden. The ground was cursed. Pain entered the world. God did not ignore their sin. And He won't ignore ours either. But in the middle of judgment… Grace appeared.

The First Covering

After Adam and Eve sinned, they tried to cover themselves.

"And they sewed fig leaves together, and made themselves aprons."

— Genesis 3:7

That's humanity's first attempt at self-righteousness. Trying to fix the problem on their own. Trying to cover sin with effort. But it wasn't enough. So God stepped in.

"Unto Adam also and to his wife did the Lord God make coats of skins, and clothed them."

— Genesis 3:21

Don't miss that. God covered them.

Grace Requires a Sacrifice

Those coats of skin didn't come from nowhere. Something had to die. This is the first picture of what grace would ultimately require: A sacrifice.

In that moment, God was showing something powerful. Sin cannot be covered by human effort. It requires something more. This was a shadow of what was coming. Because one day… Jesus would become that sacrifice.

Grace Was Already Pointing to the Cross

Even in Genesis, God was already revealing His plan. Right after the fall, He said:

"And I will put enmity between thee and the woman, and between thy seed and her seed; it shall bruise thy head, and thou shalt bruise his heel."

— Genesis 3:15

That's the first prophecy of Jesus. Right there—in the middle of humanity's failure. Grace wasn't delayed. It was immediate. God already had a plan for redemption.

The Pattern of Grace in the Old Testament

From that point forward, you see a pattern. People fail. God responds. Grace is extended. Over and over again.

Noah lived in a corrupt world.

"But Noah found grace in the eyes of the Lord."

— Genesis 6:8

Not perfection. Grace.

Abraham doubted. Moses struggled. Israel rebelled repeatedly. And yet God continued to show mercy. Why?

Because grace is not based on human consistency, it's based on God's character.

God Did Not Abandon Humanity

This is something you need to settle in your heart. God did not give up on humanity after the fall.

He didn't say, "They failed. I'm done."

He pursued. He restored. He made a way.

Grace is not God reacting. Grace is God revealing who He has always been.

What This Means for You

If grace existed at the very beginning, then your situation is not new to God. Your failure is not shocking to Him. Your struggle is not beyond Him. Your past is not too complicated for Him. He has been dealing with broken people since the beginning. And He has never stopped offering grace.

A Hard Truth

But don't misunderstand this. Just because grace is available does not mean it is automatic. Adam had to respond. Noah had to obey. Abraham had to follow. Grace invites. But you still have to answer.

The Same Call Still Stands

God is still asking the same question today:

"Where are you?"

Not because He doesn't know. But because He wants you to come out of hiding. Out of shame. Out of excuses. Out of delay. And back into a relationship with Him.

Final Thought

Grace didn't begin when you got your life together. It didn't begin when you started trying. It didn't begin when you felt worthy. Grace began the moment God chose not to give up on humanity. And that means something powerful: He hasn't given up on you either.

Chapter 3
The Difference Between Mercy and Grace

A lot of people use the words mercy and grace like they mean the same thing. They don't. They are connected—but they are not identical. And if you don't understand the difference, you won't fully understand what God has done for you.

Mercy: Not Getting What You Deserve

Let's start with mercy. Mercy is simple to define. Mercy is God withholding the punishment you deserve. You sinned. You were guilty. You deserved judgment.

But God held it back.

"It is of the Lord's mercies that we are not consumed, because his compassions fail not."

— Lamentations 3:22

That verse tells you something serious. Without mercy… we would be consumed. Mercy is the reason you're still here. Mercy is the reason judgment didn't fall immediately.

Mercy says:

"I see your sin… but I will not destroy you for it."

Grace: Receiving What You Don't Deserve

Now, grace goes further. Grace is God giving you what you do not deserve. Not just sparing you—but blessing you. Not just withholding judgment—but offering forgiveness, salvation, and relationship.

"For by grace are ye saved through faith… it is the gift of God."

— Ephesians 2:8

Grace doesn't just cancel a debt. It gives you a new life.

A Simple Way to Understand It

If you want to make it plain, remember it like this:

Mercy = You don't get what you deserve

Grace = You receive what you don't deserve

Mercy stops the punishment. Grace releases the blessing. You need both.

The Courtroom Picture

Think of it like a courtroom. You stand before a judge. You are guilty. There is no argument. No defense. No excuse. The sentence is deserved.

Now imagine this:

The judge looks at you… and chooses not to give you the punishment. That's mercy. But then, he goes further. He steps down from the bench… pays your fine himself… and sets you free. That's grace.

Now take it one step further. He doesn't just release you, he adopts you into his family.

That's the fullness of what God has done.

Why This Matters

If you only understand mercy, you will live in relief.

"If God didn't punish me, I'm okay."

But if you understand grace, you will live in transformation.

"God didn't just spare me… He changed me."

Too many people stop at mercy. They're thankful they avoided judgment, but they never step into the new life grace offers.

Mercy Without Grace Leaves You Stuck

If all you had was mercy, here's what your life would look like:

You're forgiven… but unchanged.

Spared… but still bound.

Alive… but still stuck in the same patterns.

That's not God's plan. God didn't just want to keep you out of hell. He wanted to bring you into a relationship. That's grace.

Grace Without Truth Becomes Dangerous

Now let's balance this. Some people talk about grace—but ignore truth. They say, "God loves me, so it doesn't matter how I live." That's not grace. That's distortion.

"For the grace of God that bringeth salvation hath appeared to all men, Teaching us that, denying ungodliness and worldly lusts, we should live soberly, righteously, and godly…"

— Titus 2:11–12

Grace teaches you. It corrects you. It calls you higher. If what you call "grace" is not changing how you live, it's not biblical grace.

The Cross: Where Mercy and Grace Meet

The clearest picture of both mercy and grace is the cross. Jesus didn't die so God could ignore sin. He died so sin could be paid for.

"Who his own self bare our sins in his own body on the tree…"

— 1 Peter 2:24

At the cross:

Mercy — You were not punished

Grace — Jesus was punished in your place

That's substitution. That's sacrifice. That's love at a level most people don't fully grasp.

You Didn't Earn This

This is where it gets personal. You didn't earn mercy. You didn't earn grace. You didn't clean yourself up enough to qualify. God moved first.

"But God commendeth his love toward us, in that, while we were yet sinners, Christ died for us."

— Romans 5:8

While you were still in it. Not after you fixed it.

Why Pride Struggles With This

Pride hates grace because grace removes all credit from you.

You can't say: "I saved myself."

"I figured it out."

"I earned this."

All you can say is:

"God had mercy on me…and gave me what I didn't deserve."

That humbles a man. But it also frees him.

What This Means for Your Life

If you truly understand mercy and grace, you stop trying to prove yourself. You stop pretending you're perfect. You stop living under constant guilt. But you also stop playing games with sin because you realize what it costs.

A Direct Question

Let's make this real!

Are you living like someone who has received mercy…or someone who has received grace?

Because there's a difference, one avoids punishment. The other walks in transformation.

Final Thought

God did not just spare your life. He offered you a new one. And that changes everything.

Chapter 4
Why Humanity Needs Grace

Before a person can truly receive grace, they have to face a hard truth. Something is wrong with us, not just in behavior, not just in habits, but at the core.

The Condition of Humanity

The Bible does not paint a flattering picture of human nature. It doesn't say we are "mostly good." It doesn't say we just need a little improvement. It says something much deeper.

"For all have sinned, and come short of the glory of God."

— Romans 3:23

Not some. All.

That includes: The moral person. The religious person. The person who tries to do right

No one escapes this.

Sin Is Not Just What You Do

Here's where people misunderstand. They think sin is just actions.

Lying.

Stealing.

Lusting.

Hurting others.

But sin goes deeper than behavior. Sin is a condition.

"The heart is deceitful above all things, and desperately wicked: who can know it?"

—Jeremiah 17:9

That's not surface-level. That's internal. Sin affects—your thoughts, your motives, your desires. It's not just what you do. It's what you are without God.

Why Trying Harder Doesn't Fix It

This is where most people get stuck. They try to fix themselves. They make promises.

"I'll do better."

"I'll stop this."

"I'll change."

And for a while, maybe they do, but then something happens. They fall again. Why?

Because you cannot fix a spiritual problem with human effort.

"Therefore by the deeds of the law there shall no flesh be justified…"

— Romans 3:20

Trying harder doesn't remove sin. It only exposes it.

The Cycle of Failure

This is the cycle many people live in:

Try → Fail → Feel guilty → Try again → Fail again

Over and over. And eventually, one of two things happens. Either they give up and stop trying, or they pretend they're fine and ignore the issue. Neither leads to freedom.

God's Standard Is Higher Than You Think

Another reason we need grace is this. God's standard is not human comparison.

It's perfection.

"Be ye therefore perfect, even as your Father which is in heaven is perfect."

— Matthew 5:48

That's not a suggestion. That's the standard. And if we're honest—no one meets it. Not consistently. Not completely. That's the problem.

Sin Separates You From God

Sin is not just a mistake. It creates separation.

"But your iniquities have separated between you and your God..."

— Isaiah 59:2

That's serious. God is holy. Sin cannot exist in His presence. So without grace, there is a gap between you and God that you cannot cross on your own.

The Consequence Is Real

People don't like to talk about this part. But it's the truth.

"For the wages of sin is death..."

— Romans 6:23

Sin pays a wage, and that wage is death, not just physical death but spiritual separation from God. This is why grace is not optional. It is necessary.

Why Good Works Aren't Enough

Many people believe: "If I do enough good, it will balance out the bad."

But that's not how it works.

"But we are all as an unclean thing, and all our righteousnesses are as filthy rags..."

— Isaiah 64:6

Even your best efforts fall short. That doesn't mean good works are meaningless. It means they are not enough to save you.

Religion Cannot Save You

This is another hard truth. Religion alone cannot fix the problem. You can go to church, read Scripture, and say prayers. And still not be transformed. Why? Because the issue is not external, it's internal. And only grace can reach that level.

This Is Why Grace Matters

Now you see it clearly. Without grace, sin remains, guilt remains, separation remains. Grace is not an extra. It is the only solution.

"...but the gift of God is eternal life through Jesus Christ our Lord."

— Romans 6:23

That's the second half of the verse. That's the hope.

Grace Is Rescue, Not Assistance

Let's make this clear. Grace is not God helping you improve. Grace is God rescuing you.

You are not a good person who needs a boost. You are a broken person who needs saving.

That may sound strong, but it's the truth that leads to freedom.

A Personal Question

Let's bring this to you directly: Have you recognized your need for grace?

Not intellectually. Personally. Because until you see the depth of the problem, you won't fully appreciate the solution.

Final Thought

Grace only makes sense when you understand what it's saving you from. And once you truly understand that… you will never take it lightly again.

Chapter 5
Grace Revealed Through Jesus Christ

Grace is not just an idea. It's not just a concept. Grace is a person, and His name is Jesus Christ.

The Law Revealed the Problem—Jesus Brought the Solution

Before Jesus came, God gave the law. The law showed people what was right and what was wrong. It revealed sin. But it didn't remove it.

"For the law was given by Moses, but grace and truth came by Jesus Christ."

—John 1:17

The law says, "This is what you must do."

Grace says, "This is what has been done for you."

That's the difference.

Jesus Didn't Come for the Righteous

One of the most misunderstood things about Jesus is who He came for. People assume He came for the "good." The religious. The disciplined. The morally upright. But Jesus said something very different.

"They that be whole need not a physician, but they that are sick.

I came not to call the righteous, but sinners to repentance."

— Luke 5:31–32

That changes everything. Grace is not for those who think they're fine.

It's for those who know they're not.

He Stepped Into Our Condition

Jesus didn't stay distant. He stepped into the brokenness of humanity. He saw: the pain, the sin, the rejection, the suffering, and He didn't turn away.

"And the Word was made flesh, and dwelt among us…"

—John 1:14

God came down. Not to condemn first, but to reach.

Grace in Action

Look at how Jesus lived. He touched lepers that others avoided. He spoke to outcasts whom others rejected. He forgave people whom others condemned. One of the most powerful moments was when a woman caught in adultery was brought before Him. The law demanded her death. The crowd was ready. But Jesus responded:

"He that is without sin among you, let him first cast a stone…"

—John 8:7

One by one, they walked away. Then Jesus said:

"Neither do I condemn thee: go, and sin no more."

—John 8:11

That is grace and truth together. Not condemnation. But not permission either. Forgiveness… followed by a call to change.

The Cross Was Not an Accident

Now we come to the center of it all—the cross. Jesus didn't just teach grace. He paid for it.

"And being found in fashion as a man, he humbled himself, and became obedient unto death, even the death of the cross."

— Philippians 2:8

This was not random. This was intentional. Jesus knew what was coming. And He chose it.

Substitution: The Heart of Grace

Here is the truth that defines everything. Jesus took your place.

"For he hath made him to be sin for us, who knew no sin; that we might be made the righteousness of God in him."

— 2 Corinthians 5:21

Think about that. He had no sin, but He took yours. So you could receive what you didn't earn. That's grace at its deepest level.

Justice Was Satisfied

God did not ignore sin. He judged it. But instead of judging you, He placed that judgment on Jesus.

"Who his own self bare our sins in his own body on the tree..."

— 1 Peter 2:24

Every failure. Every lie. Every hidden sin. Paid for, not dismissed. Paid.

Love Proven, Not Just Spoken

A lot of people say, "God loves me."

But the cross proves it.

"But God commendeth his love toward us, in that, while we were yet sinners, Christ died for us."

— Romans 5:8

Not when you got it right. Not when you cleaned up your life. While you were still in it. That's not weak love. That's sacrificial love.

The Resurrection Confirms It

Grace didn't end at the cross. Jesus didn't stay in the grave.

He rose.

"He is not here: for he is risen..."

— Matthew 28:6

That matters because it proves that sin was defeated. Death was overcome The payment was accepted. Grace is not just offered. It is secured.

Why Jesus Is the Only Way

This is where people push back. They want grace—but not Jesus. They want forgiveness—but not surrender. But Scripture is clear:

"Jesus saith unto him, I am the way, the truth, and the life: no man cometh unto the Father, but by me."

—John 14:6

There is no alternate path. No backup plan. Grace flows through Christ.

You Can't Earn What He Already Paid For

Here's the mistake many people make. They try to add to what Jesus already did. They think, "I need to do more."

"I need to prove myself."

"I need to earn this."

You can't. If you could, the cross wouldn't have been necessary. Grace is received. Not achieved.

A Personal Question

Let's bring it to you again. What have you done with Jesus? Not what you think about Him.

Not what you've heard. What have you done with Him? Because everything about grace depends on that answer.

Final Thought

Grace is not a vague idea floating in the background. It has a name. It has a face. It has a cross. And it has an invitation. Jesus Christ is that invitation.

Chapter 6
Grace for the Worst Sinners

There are people who believe in grace, but not for themselves.

They hear that God forgives. They see others change. They understand the message. But deep down, they think:

"Not me."

"You don't know what I've done."

"I've crossed a line I can't come back from."

Let's deal with that directly. That is a lie.

Where That Thought Comes From

That thought doesn't come from God. It comes from guilt, shame, and the enemy.

Because if you can be convinced you're too far gone, you'll never come back.

And if you never come back, you stay exactly where you are.

What Scripture Actually Says

The Bible doesn't say:

"Grace is available for those who haven't messed up too badly."

It says:

"Where sin abounded, grace did much more abound."

— Romans 5:20

Not equal. More. That means no matter how deep sin goes, grace goes deeper.

David — A Man Who Fell Hard

David wasn't just a sinner. He committed adultery. Then arranged the death of a man to cover it. That's not a small failure. That's serious. And yet, when David repented, God forgave him.

"I acknowledge my transgressions... Against thee, thee only, have I sinned..."

— Psalm 51:3–4

David didn't excuse it. He owned it. And grace met him there.

Paul — From Persecutor to Apostle

Before Paul preached the Gospel, He hunted Christians.

"Who was before a blasphemer, and a persecutor, and injurious... but I obtained mercy..."

— 1 Timothy 1:13

He approved of their deaths. He was actively working against God. And God didn't destroy him. He transformed him. That's grace.

The Thief on the Cross

Now look at one of the clearest examples. A man who lived a life of crime was dying next to Jesus. There was no time to fix his past. No time to prove anything. No second chances and yet—he turned to Jesus and said:

"Lord, remember me when thou comest into thy kingdom."

— Luke 23:42

And Jesus responded:

"Today shalt thou be with me in paradise."

— Luke 23:43

In a moment—Grace covered a lifetime.

Let that sink in. That man did not earn anything. He didn't: make restitution, live a better life, or prove his sincerity over time. He only believed, and he surrendered. And that was enough.

The Real Issue Isn't Your Past

Here's what you need to understand: Your past is not what keeps you from God. Your refusal to come back is. God already knows everything you've done. Nothing about your life surprises Him. The issue is not:

"Have you sinned too much?"

The issue is:

"Will you turn back?"

Shame Keeps You Stuck

Shame is one of the enemy's strongest tools.

It tells you: "Hide."

"Stay away."

"You don't belong anymore."

But grace says the opposite:

"Come back."

"Come now."

"Don't wait."

"Let us therefore come boldly unto the throne of grace..."

— Hebrews 4:16

Not hiding. Boldly. Even when you feel unworthy.

There Is Only One Unforgivable Direction

Let's make this clear:

There is no sin too big for grace. But there is a condition. You must come to God. The only place where grace is not received is where it is rejected.

Stop Measuring Your Sin Against Others

Another trap people fall into: Comparison.

They think: "At least I'm not as bad as them..."

Or: "I'm worse than everyone else..."

Both are wrong. Grace is not based on comparison. It's based on Christ.

You Are Not the Exception

Some people think they are the one exception.

"The Bible applies to everyone else... just not me."

No. You are not beyond grace. You are exactly who grace was made for.

But Don't Misunderstand This

Now hear this clearly: Grace being available does not mean sin is casual. Sin still destroys. Sin still wounds. Sin still has consequences. Grace forgives. But it also calls you out of it.

A Direct Question

Let's bring it straight to you:

What are you still holding onto that makes you feel disqualified?

What mistake?

What pattern?

What past decision?

Now ask yourself this:

Are you going to let that keep you from God…or bring it to Him?

Final Thought

Grace is not for people who almost got it right. It's for people who know they didn't. And if you're honest—that includes all of us.

Chapter 7
Grace in the Middle of Failure and Relapse

Let's be honest.

Some of the hardest moments in a believer's life are not before coming to God… they're after.

Because before you knew better, you lived how you lived. But after? You knew. You prayed.

You meant it. And then you fell again.

The Weight of Repeated Failure

There's a different kind of pain that comes with relapse.

Not just guilt, but disappointment.

You think, *"I said I wouldn't do this again."*

"I asked God to help me."

"I thought I was past this."

And now you're right back where you were. That hits differently.

This Is Where Many People Give Up

This is the moment where many people start to drift. Not all at once. Slowly. They stop praying like they used to. They avoid Scripture. They feel like hypocrites. And eventually, they begin to believe: "What's the point?"

Paul Understood This Struggle

This isn't new. Even Paul wrestled with it.

"For the good that I would I do not: but the evil which I would not, that I do."

— Romans 7:19

That's not a weak man speaking. That's an honest one. There is a battle inside you.

And sometimes—it's intense.

The Difference Between Struggle and Surrender

Now this is critical to understand: There is a difference between struggling with sin… and surrendering to it.

Struggle means: You fight.

You resist.

You care.

Surrender means: You accept it.

You justify it. You stop trying.

If you're still fighting—even if you're losing sometimes—that matters.

Failure Does Not Cancel Grace

Here's the truth you need to hold onto: Failure does not cancel grace. If it did, no one would make it.

"My little children, these things write I unto you, that ye sin not.

And if any man sin, we have an advocate with the Father, Jesus Christ the righteous."

— 1 John 2:1

Notice that:

Not if someone perfects themselves. But if any man sin. There is still a provision.

Conviction vs Condemnation

You need to learn the difference between the two voices:

Conviction (from God):

"That's not who you are anymore."

"Get back up."

"Come back to Me."

Condemnation (not from God):

"You'll never change."

"You've failed too many times."

"Just stay down."

"There is therefore now no condemnation to them which are in Christ Jesus…"

— Romans 8:1

Condemnation pushes you away. Conviction pulls you back.

Why Relapse Happens

Let's not ignore reality. Relapse doesn't just happen randomly. There are patterns. Triggers.

Weak moments. Unaddressed habits.

Jesus said:

"The spirit indeed is willing, but the flesh is weak."

— Matthew 26:41

Your desire to change may be real.

But if you don't deal with the areas of weakness, you will keep falling into them.

Grace Is Not Passive—It Strengthens You

Some people treat grace like it just forgives and moves on. But grace does more than that.

"Let us therefore come boldly unto the throne of grace, that we may obtain mercy, and find grace to help in time of need."

— Hebrews 4:16

Grace helps. Grace strengthens. Grace equips you to fight differently.

You Have to Get Back Up Quickly

One of the biggest mistakes people make after failure: They stay down too long. They wait until they "feel right" again. They distance themselves from God.

That's the wrong move. The moment you fall—come back. Immediately. Not after a week.

Not after you fix yourself. Now.

Stop Trying to Hide It

Going back to the beginning— Adam hid.

And we still do the same. We hide failure behind silence. But healing doesn't happen in hiding.

"He that covereth his sins shall not prosper: but whoso confesseth and forsaketh them shall have mercy."

— Proverbs 28:13

Bring it into the light. That's where grace works.

Progress, Not Perfection

You are not going to be perfect overnight. Growth takes time. But there should be movement. Less frequency. Less control. More awareness.

Grace doesn't produce instant perfection, but it produces direction.

A Hard Truth

If you keep excusing what God is trying to remove, you will stay stuck. Grace forgives failure. But it does not support rebellion. There has to be a point where you say,

"I don't want this anymore."

Even if you're still struggling.

A Direct Question

What is the thing you keep going back to? Be honest. Not generally. Specifically. Because vague repentance produces vague change. But clarity leads to a breakthrough.

Final Thought

You are not disqualified because you fell. You are only disqualified if you refuse to get back up. Grace is still there. Not waiting for a better version of you, but calling you back right now.

Chapter 8
Grace That Transforms

There is a version of grace being talked about today that is not biblical. It sounds comforting. It sounds accepting. It sounds easy. But it does not change anything. And if it doesn't change anything—it's not real grace.

The Danger of Misunderstood Grace

Some people hear about grace and think:

"I'm forgiven, so it doesn't matter how I live."

"God knows my heart."

"No one's perfect."

And they use those statements as a shield. Not to grow—but to stay the same. That's not grace. That's avoidance.

Paul Confronts This Directly

This isn't a new problem. Even in the early church, people twisted grace. So Paul addressed it clearly:

"What shall we say then? Shall we continue in sin, that grace may abound? God forbid."

— Romans 6:1–2

That phrase—God forbid—is strong. It means: Absolutely not. No way. That is not what grace is for.

Grace Breaks Chains

Real grace does not make sin comfortable. It breaks its hold.

"For sin shall not have dominion over you: for ye are not under the law, but under grace."

— Romans 6:14

Notice that: Grace doesn't increase sin's control. It destroys it. If something still has complete control over your life, grace is not being applied there yet.

Transformation Starts on the Inside

Change doesn't begin with behavior. It begins with the heart.

"Therefore if any man be in Christ, he is a new creature: old things are passed away; behold, all things are become new."

— 2 Corinthians 5:17

That doesn't mean instant perfection. But it does mean: You are no longer the same person.

Your identity changes. And over time, your life follows.

Grace Changes What You Want

This is one of the biggest signs of real grace: Your desires begin to shift. Things you once justified start to bother you. Things you once pursued start to lose their pull. Not because someone forced you but because something inside you changed.

You Can't Stay Comfortable in Sin

If you can live in sin without conviction—something is wrong. Because grace teaches.

"For the grace of God that bringeth salvation hath appeared to all men, Teaching us that, denying ungodliness and worldly lusts, we should live soberly, righteously, and godly…"

— Titus 2:11–12

Grace doesn't ignore sin. It trains you to walk away from it.

Excuses Keep You Stuck

Let's deal with something honestly. Excuses will keep you bound.

"I've always been this way."

"It's just how I am."

"I'll deal with it later."

Those are not reasons. They are barriers. Grace is available, but you still have to respond.

Surrender Is the Turning Point Transformation begins at surrender; not partial surrender; not conditional surrender.

Full surrender.

"I beseech you therefore, brethren… that ye present your bodies a living sacrifice, holy, acceptable unto God…"

— Romans 12:1

A sacrifice doesn't negotiate. It yields. That's where change starts.

Grace Gives You Power to Say No

You are not left alone in this. Grace empowers you.

"I can do all things through Christ which strengtheneth me."

— Philippians 4:13

That includes saying no to things that used to control you. Not perfectly, but increasingly.

Transformation Is a Process

Now be clear: This doesn't happen overnight.

There will be: Struggles, growth seasons, and setbacks.

But direction matters more than speed. If you are moving toward God—that's transformation in motion.

A Hard Line

Here's where we draw it clearly. If nothing in your life is changing, you don't need more information. But instead, you need a real encounter with grace. Because real grace leaves evidence.

A Personal Question

Let's make it real again:

What in your life has not changed? Not what you talk about. Not what you intend.

What has actually remained the same?

Now ask yourself: Have you truly surrendered that to God?

Final Thought

Grace is not there to make you comfortable in sin. It is there to free you from it, and freedom always requires movement.

Chapter 9
Living Daily in God's Grace

It's one thing to have a moment with God; it's another thing to walk with Him daily.

A lot of people experience grace once and then spend the rest of their lives trying to figure out how to maintain it. They go back and forth between: Feeling close to God... then distant... then trying again... then falling off. That cycle is exhausting, and it's not how this is supposed to work.

Grace Is Not Just a Moment—It's a Way of Life

Grace is not just what saves you, it's what sustains you.

"As ye have therefore received Christ Jesus the Lord, so walk ye in him."

— Colossians 2:6

How did you receive Him? By grace and through faith. That's how you continue, not by suddenly switching to self-effort.

Stop Trying to Earn What Was Given

This is where many people drift. They start thinking:

"I need to prove I'm worthy now."

"I need to do enough to stay right with God."

So they begin striving, trying harder, and doing more. They begin carrying pressure, but that leads to burnout because you cannot maintain by effort what was given by grace.

Grace Produces Relationship, Not Performance

God didn't save you to put you on a performance system. He saved you for a relationship.

"Abide in me, and I in you..."

—John 15:4

The word "abide" means to stay connected. Remain. Live in that relationship. Not visit occasionally.

Daily Dependence

Living in grace means daily dependence on God. Not just in crisis, not just when you fail.

Every day.

"Give us this day our daily bread."

— Matthew 6:11

Daily. Not weekly. Not occasionally. You need Him every day.

Grace in Your Thoughts

Your mind matters. A lot of people receive grace, but still think like they're condemned.

They replay failures. They carry guilt. They expect rejection.

But Scripture says:

"Be ye transformed by the renewing of your mind..."

— Romans 12:2

Grace doesn't just change your standing. It changes how you think.

Grace When You Mess Up

Let's be real—you're going to have moments. Bad days. Wrong reactions. Failures.

The question is:

What do you do next? Do you pull away? Or do you come back immediately?

"If we confess our sins, he is faithful and just to forgive us…"

— 1 John 1:9

That's daily grace, not a one-time offer.

Consistency Over Emotion

Here's something important: Your walk with God cannot be based on how you feel. Some days you'll feel close. Some days you won't. But grace is not based on emotion.

It's based on truth. Stay consistent even when you don't feel it. That's maturity.

Building Daily Habits

Living in grace doesn't mean doing nothing. It means doing the right things from the right place. Not to earn God's favor, but because you already have it. Remember, daily habits matter:

- Prayer
- Scripture
- Quiet reflection
- Obedience in small things

These are not burdens. They are lifelines.

Grace and Discipline Work Together

Some people think grace removes discipline. It doesn't. It gives purpose to it.

"For whom the Lord loveth he chasteneth…"

— Hebrews 12:6

God corrects you because He loves you. Not to push you away, but to guide you forward.

You Won't Always Get It Right

Let's remove unrealistic expectations. You are not going to:

- Always say the right thing
- Always respond perfectly
- Always stay consistent

But you can stay committed. That's the difference.

Stay Close, Not Perfect

The goal is not perfection. The goal is closeness and stay near God.

"Draw nigh to God, and he will draw nigh to you…"

—James 4:8

That's a promise. And it applies daily.

A Personal Question

Let's make it practical:

What does your daily walk with God actually look like right now? Not what you want it to be.

Not what it used to be. Right now. Is it consistent? Or occasional?

Final Thought

Grace is not just what brought you to God. It's what keeps you walking with Him. Every day. Step by step.

Chapter 10
Grace and Forgiving Others

It's easy to ask God for forgiveness. It's much harder to give it to someone who hurt you.

Because when pain is personal… Grace becomes costly.

The Standard Is Clear

Scripture doesn't leave this open to interpretation:

"And be ye kind one to another, tenderhearted, forgiving one another, even as God for Christ's sake hath forgiven you."

— Ephesians 4:32

That last part matters:

"…even as God… hath forgiven you."

That's the standard. Not how you feel. Not what they deserve. How God forgave you.

Why This Is So Difficult

Let's be honest. Some wounds run deep, such as betrayal, abandonment, lies, and broken trust. And when someone causes real pain, something inside you says: "They don't deserve forgiveness."

And you're right, they don't. But neither did you, and that's what makes it grace.

Forgiveness Is Not Saying It Was Okay

This is where people get confused. Forgiveness is not about saying what happened didn't matter, pretending it didn't hurt, or calling wrong "right." Forgiveness acknowledges the wrong, but chooses not to hold it against them.

Unforgiveness Keeps You Bound

A lot of people think unforgiveness punishes the other person. It doesn't; it traps you. You replay the moment. You carry the weight. You relive the pain over and over.

"For if ye forgive men their trespasses, your heavenly Father will also forgive you: But if ye forgive not men… neither will your Father forgive your trespasses."

— Matthew 6:14–15

That's serious. Unforgiveness doesn't just affect relationships, but it also affects your connection with God.

You Cannot Receive and Refuse at the Same Time

Here's the hard truth:

You cannot fully receive grace while refusing to give it because grace flows. It's not meant to stop with you.

Jesus Modeled This on the Cross

Think about this moment: Jesus is being crucified, mocked, beaten and killed. And what does He say?

"Father, forgive them; for they know not what they do."

— Luke 23:34

That's not theory. That's reality. If anyone had the right to hold offense, it was Him. And He still chose forgiveness.

Forgiveness Is a Decision, Not a Feeling

You may not feel ready. You may not feel peace about it. But forgiveness is not based on feeling. It's a decision. A choice you make—sometimes daily. Feelings will follow later, but the decision comes first.

You Don't Need Their Apology

Another trap:

"I'll forgive them when they apologize."

What if they never do? What if they don't care? What if they don't even think they were wrong? If your freedom depends on their response, you stay stuck. Forgiveness is something you do between you and God, not you and them.

Boundaries Still Matter

Now hear this clearly:

Forgiveness does not mean that trust is automatically restored. You allow the same behavior again. You remove all boundaries. You can forgive someone and still be wise about access to your life.

God Heals What You Release

There are wounds God wants to heal, but you keep reopening them by holding onto offense. When you release it healing begins. Not instantly, but genuinely.

A Personal Question

Let's make this real: Who have you not forgiven? Not generally, specifically.

What name comes to mind right now? That's where grace needs to go next.

A Hard Step

You may need to say something like this:

"God, they hurt me.

And it wasn't okay.

But I release it.

I choose to forgive."

Not because they deserve it, but because you were forgiven.

Final Thought

Grace changed your standing with God. Now it's meant to change how you treat others. And sometimes, the person you need to release is the very thing standing between you and deeper freedom.

Chapter 11
Grace in the Middle of Suffering

There are moments in life that shake you, moments you didn't expect, didn't plan for, didn't want. Loss. Pain. Disappointment. Waiting.

And in those moments, a question rises up:

"Where is God in this?"

Grace Doesn't Always Remove the Pain

This is where people get confused. They think grace means:

"No problems."

"No suffering."

"No hardship."

But that's not what Scripture teaches. Sometimes grace doesn't remove the storm—it carries you through it.

Paul's Thorn

Paul prayed for something to be removed. Not once. Not casually. Three times.

And God's answer was not what he expected:

"My grace is sufficient for thee: for my strength is made perfect in weakness."

— 2 Corinthians 12:9

God didn't remove the struggle. He gave strength in the middle of it.

Strength Looks Different Than You Think

We tend to define strength as:

Winning.

Overcoming quickly.

Avoiding pain.

But God defines it differently. Strength is: enduring, trusting and staying faithful when it's hard. Grace gives you that kind of strength.

Suffering Reveals What's Inside

Pressure exposes things. When life is easy, it's simple to say you trust God. But when things fall apart, what's really in your heart comes to the surface.

Fear. Doubt. Anger. Or faith.

God Is Still Present

One of the biggest lies during suffering is this:

"God has left me."

But Scripture says otherwise:

"I will never leave thee, nor forsake thee."

— Hebrews 13:5

Never. Even when you don't feel it. Even when it's quiet. Even when nothing makes sense.

Jesus Understands Suffering

You are not following a distant God. Jesus suffered. He was rejected, betrayed, beaten and crucified.

"A man of sorrows, and acquainted with grief…"

— Isaiah 53:3

He knows what pain feels like which means when you suffer he understands.

Grace Keeps You From Breaking

Some people look back and say:

"I don't know how I made it through that."

That's grace.

Holding you together when you should have fallen apart. Carrying you when you had no strength left.

Not All Pain Is Punishment

This is important. Every hardship is not God punishing you. Sometimes, it's life in a broken world. It's the result of others' choices. It's a season of growth. Don't assume every struggle means God is against you.

God Uses What He Doesn't Remove

Even when God doesn't take something away—He can use it.

"And we know that all things work together for good to them that love God…"

— Romans 8:28

Not some things, all things. Even pain. Even loss. Even the things you wouldn't choose.

Waiting Is Part of Suffering

Sometimes the pain isn't an event. It's the waiting. Waiting for answers, healing, change, breakthrough. And in that waiting, faith is tested.

Grace in the Waiting

Grace sustains you when nothing is happening. When prayers feel unanswered. When progress feels slow. When you don't see the outcome yet. That's where real trust grows.

Don't Let Pain Push You Away

This is where many people make a critical mistake. They pull away from God during suffering. They get quiet. Distant. Disconnected. But that's when you need Him most.

Run to Him—not away.

A Personal Question

Let's make this real:

What are you carrying right now? What pain, what situation, what burden… have you brought it to God honestly? Or have you been trying to carry it alone?

Final Thought

Grace is not just for when you fail. It's for when you hurt. And sometimes, the greatest evidence of grace… is that you're still standing.

Chapter 12
Grace in the Last Days

We are not just living in ordinary times. Something is shifting. You can see it:

In the world

In culture

In people

Things that were once called wrong are now celebrated. Truth is being blurred. Conviction is fading. And many people feel it: Something isn't right.

Scripture Warned This Would Happen

None of this is new to God.

It was already written:

"This know also, that in the last days perilous times shall come."

— 2 Timothy 3:1

And then it describes people: Lovers of self, lovers of pleasure more than lovers of God, having a form of godliness, but denying the power. That sounds familiar.

A Form Without Power

This is one of the most dangerous conditions:

Looking like you have faith, but lacking real transformation.

People talk about God, quote Scripture, identify as believers, but there is no change. No conviction. No surrender. No power.

That's not grace. That's appearance.

Grace Is Being Distorted

In the last days, even grace is misunderstood.

"Turning the grace of our God into lasciviousness…"

—Jude 1:4

That means using grace as an excuse for sin. Calling compromise "freedom." Calling disobedience "grace." That's deception.

Truth Is Being Replaced

Another sign: Truth becomes optional.

"For the time will come when they will not endure sound doctrine…"

— 2 Timothy 4:3

People don't want truth anymore. They want comfort. They want messages that don't confront them. That don't challenge them. That don't require change.

Why This Matters for You

This is not just about the world. It's about you. Because it's easy to get pulled into this without realizing it. To slowly compromise. To slowly drift. To slowly become comfortable.

Grace is not meant to make you blend in. It's meant to set you apart.

Stay Awake

Jesus said it clearly:

"Watch therefore: for ye know not what hour your Lord doth come."

— Matthew 24:42

Stay alert. Spiritually awake. Not distracted. Not passive. Engaged.

Grace Is Still Available—But Time Matters

Here's something people don't like to think about: Grace has a window. Not because God is unwilling but because life is limited.

"Now is the accepted time; behold, now is the day of salvation."

— 2 Corinthians 6:2

Now. Not later. Not someday. Now.

Don't Delay What Matters Most

A dangerous mindset is this:

"I'll deal with that later."

"I'll get serious eventually."

But time is not guaranteed and delay hardens the heart.

The longer you wait, the easier it becomes to ignore.

Grace Calls for Readiness

Grace is not just about forgiveness. It's about preparation. Being ready:

In your faith

In your life

In your heart

Not perfect, but positioned.

You Can't Follow the Crowd

In the last days, following the crowd will lead you the wrong way. Because the majority won't choose truth.

"Enter ye in at the strait gate… because strait is the gate, and narrow is the way, which leadeth unto life, and few there be that find it."

— Matthew 7:13–14

Few. That means you have to be intentional.

Stay Grounded in the Word

Your foundation matters. Feelings will shift, culture will change, opinions will vary. But God's Word doesn't. That's where you stay anchored.

A Personal Question

Let's bring this to you:

Are you drifting… or are you standing firm? Be honest. Because small compromises lead to bigger ones. And before you know it, you're somewhere you never intended to be.

Final Thought

Grace is still reaching. Still calling. Still available. But the time to respond… is now.

Chapter 13
When Grace Is Rejected

Grace is freely given, but it is not forced. God offers it. He extends it. He calls people toward it. But He does not make the decision for them.

Grace Can Be Refused

This is something many people don't want to accept. They assume:

"If God is loving, everyone will be saved."

But Scripture doesn't teach that, because love gives a choice. And a choice means the possibility of rejection.

A Dangerous Pattern

Rejection of grace rarely happens all at once. It's usually gradual. A person hears truth… and ignores it. Feels conviction… and pushes it away. Knows they should respond… and delays. Over time, something happens. The heart hardens.

The Heart Can Become Hardened

"Today if ye will hear his voice, harden not your hearts…"

— Hebrews 3:15

That warning exists for a reason, because every time you resist truth. It becomes easier to resist the next time. Conviction fades. Sensitivity dulls. And what once bothered you… doesn't anymore.

Familiarity Without Surrender

Another form of rejection is this: Being around truth… but never responding to it.

You can: Hear messages, read Scripture, talk about God and still never surrender.

That's dangerous, because it creates the illusion of being right with God—without actually being right.

The Rich Young Ruler

There was a man who came to Jesus. He asked the right question:

"What shall I do that I may inherit eternal life?"

— Mark 10:17

Jesus answered him directly. But when it came time to surrender. He walked away.

Why? Because he didn't want to let go of what he was holding onto. He was close, but not surrendered.

Almost Is Not Enough

This is a hard truth: Almost following God… is still rejecting Him. Almost surrendering… is still holding back. Almost choosing grace… is still saying no. And almost does not save you.

The Cost of Rejection

Grace is a gift, but rejecting it has consequences.

"He that believeth not shall be damned."

— Mark 16:16

That's not popular. But it's truth. God doesn't send people away without reason. People choose not to come.

God Is Patient—But Not Indefinitely

God is patient. He gives opportunities. He calls repeatedly. But patience is not endless delay.

"The Lord is not slack concerning his promise… but is longsuffering… not willing that any should perish…"

— 2 Peter 3:9

God desires people to come. But He will not override their will.

What Rejection Looks Like Today

Rejection doesn't always look obvious. It can look like:

"I'll deal with that later."

"I'm not ready yet."

"I believe… but I'm not changing."

That's still rejection, because grace requires a response.

You Don't Stay Neutral

There is no neutral position with God, you are either moving toward Him or away from Him.

Silence is a decision. Delay is a decision. Ignoring is a decision.

A Personal Question

Let's make this direct:

Have you been putting off what you know you need to do?

Not unsure. Not confused. You know.

And you've been delaying it.

Why?

This Is the Moment That Matters

Every time you hear truth, you have a choice. To respond, or to resist.

And those choices shape your heart over time.

Final Thought

Grace is one of the greatest gifts ever given. But a gift only matters… if it's received.

Chapter 14
The Invitation of Grace

After all the truth, after all the conviction, after everything that's been exposed—there is still an invitation. Not rejection. Not distance. Not "come back when you're better." An invitation.

God Is Still Calling

No matter what you've read so far… no matter what you've done, God is still calling you.

"Come unto me, all ye that labour and are heavy laden, and I will give you rest."

— Matthew 11:28

Not the perfect. Not the cleaned-up. The weary. The burdened. The ones carrying weight.

You Don't Have to Fix Yourself First

This is where people hesitate. They think:

"I need to get my life together first."

"I need to fix some things before I come back."

No.

If you could fix yourself—you wouldn't need grace. Grace is what meets you before you change. Not after.

The Door Is Open Right Now

Grace is not waiting on a future version of you. It's available right now. Not when you feel ready. Not when everything lines up. Now.

"Behold, I stand at the door, and knock..."

— Revelation 3:20

That's not forced entry. That's invitation.

God Wants Relationship—Not Religion

This is not about: Following rules perfectly, performing religious duties, looking like you have it together. God wants you. Your heart. Your honesty. Your surrender.

The Prodigal Son

One of the clearest pictures of grace is found here. A son walked away from his father. Wasted everything. Made a mess of his life. And then decided to come back. Not proud. Not confident. Broken. And what happened?

"But when he was yet a great way off, his father saw him... and had compassion, and ran..."

— Luke 15:20

The father didn't wait. He ran. That's grace.

You Are Not Too Far Gone

Let's say it again clearly: You are not too far gone. Not because of what you've done. Not because of how long it's been. Not because of how many times you've failed. Grace is still reaching.

But You Must Respond

Here's the part that matters. An invitation requires a response. You can hear it. Understand it. Even agree with it. And still walk away. Just like the rich young ruler. Grace is offered. But you must receive it.

What It Means to Come to God

It's not complicated. It's honest. It's saying:

"I need You."

"I can't fix this on my own."

"I surrender."

That's where it starts.

Faith and Surrender

"That if thou shalt confess with thy mouth the Lord Jesus, and shalt believe in thine heart… thou shalt be saved."

— Romans 10:9

Believe.

Confess.

Surrender.

Not perfectly.

But genuinely.

This Is Personal

This is not about what someone else thinks. What others expect. What your past says.

This is between you and God. Right now.

A Direct Question

Are you ready to respond?

Not later. Not eventually. Now. Because you've heard the truth. You've felt conviction. You've seen what grace is. So what will you do with it?

Final Thought

Grace is standing at the door. Not forcing. Not demanding. But calling. And all that remains… is your answer.

Final Chapter
A Life Transformed by Grace

By now, you've seen what grace is. You've seen: The truth about sin. The reality of failure. The power of the cross. The invitation to come back. But none of that matters until it becomes real in your life.

Grace Changes More Than Your Status

Grace doesn't just change where you stand with God. It changes who you are becoming.

Too many people stop at forgiveness.

"I'm forgiven, so I'm good."

But grace goes further than that. It transforms.

A New Identity

When grace takes hold, you are no longer defined by your past. Not your mistakes. Not your failures. Not your worst decisions.

"Therefore if any man be in Christ, he is a new creature…"

— 2 Corinthians 5:17

That's not symbolic. That's real. You are not the same person anymore.

The Old Life Loses Its Grip

Things that once controlled you begin to lose their power.

Not instantly.

Not perfectly.

But gradually.

Because grace doesn't just forgive sin, it breaks its hold.

You Begin to Walk Differently

Your choices start to change. Your priorities shift. Your perspective becomes clearer. Not because you're trying to impress God, but because something inside you has changed.

You See Others Differently

Grace doesn't just affect how you see yourself. It changes how you see people.

You become:

More patient

More compassionate

Less judgmental

Because you remember what God brought you out of.

You Stop Living for Yourself

This is where transformation becomes visible. Your life stops being centered on you.

"And that he died for all, that they which live should not henceforth live unto themselves…"

— 2 Corinthians 5:15

Grace shifts your focus. From self to God.

You Still Face Battles

Let's be clear. Transformation does not mean: No struggles. No temptations. No difficult days. You will still face things. But you won't face them the same way. Because now—you're not alone.

Grace Keeps You Grounded

As your life changes, there's a danger: Pride.

Thinking: "I've come a long way."

"I'm doing better than others."

But grace reminds you: Everything you are, is because of God.

"But by the grace of God I am what I am…"

— 1 Corinthians 15:10

That keeps you humble.

You Start Living With Purpose

Grace doesn't just save you from something. It calls you to something. Your life begins to have direction. Meaning. Purpose. Not just existing, but living intentionally.

You Become a Reflection

This is where it becomes powerful. Your life starts reflecting grace to others.

People see:

The change

The growth

The difference

Not perfection—

But evidence.

And that points them to God.

A Life That Continues to Grow

Transformation is not a one-time event. It's ongoing. Day by day. Step by step. You keep growing. Keep learning. Keep becoming.

A Final Question Before the Call

Now it comes down to this:

Do you want this? Not the idea of it. Not the appearance of it. The real thing. A life changed by grace.

Final Thought

Grace is not just something you hear about. It's something you live in. And when it truly takes hold of your life, everything changes.

Altar Call
A Moment That Cannot Be Ignored

If you've read this far, this is not an accident. You didn't just come across these words randomly. God has been speaking to you. Through conviction. Through truth. Through that quiet voice inside you that keeps saying:

"Something needs to change."

This Is Your Moment

Right now, you have a choice. Not tomorrow. Not someday. Right now.

You've heard the truth about grace. You've seen what sin does. You've felt conviction. So the question is not:

"Do I understand?"

The question is:

"Will I respond?"

Stop running. You already know. You've felt it —the pull. The conviction. The awareness that you're not where you should be. And maybe you've tried to ignore it. Maybe you've said: *"I'll deal with this later."*

"I'm not ready yet."

But listen carefully:

There is no safer moment than this one.

You Don't Need to Clean Yourself Up

Somewhere along the way, you may have believed:

"I need to fix myself first."

No.

You come as you are.

Broken.

Guilty.

Honest.

That's exactly who grace is for.

What God Is Asking From You

Not perfection. Not performance. Just this: Surrender.

Let go of trying to control everything. Let go of holding onto what's been pulling you down. Let go of the delay. And come to Him.

This Is Between You and God

Not your past. Not other people. Not your reputation. This is personal right now, wherever you are.

A Simple Prayer of Surrender

If you're ready to stop running. If you're ready to come back. If you're ready to give your life to God, pray this honestly:

"God… I know I've sinned. I know I've gone my own way. And I can't fix this on my own. I believe Jesus Christ died for my sins… and rose again.

Right now, I turn back to You. I surrender my life to You. Forgive me. Change me. Make me new. I give You my life—fully. In Jesus' name… Amen."

If You Meant That

If you prayed that—and you meant it—something just changed. Not because of perfect words. But because of a real decision.

Now Don't Go Back

This is where it begins, not where it ends. Start walking with God, pray daily, read His Word, stay connected, and when you stumble, get back up quickly.

Final Words

You were not too far gone. You were not forgotten. And it was not too late. Grace was reaching for you. And today is your chance to accept it!

www.ingramcontent.com/pod-product-compliance
Lightning Source LLC
Chambersburg PA
CBHW051237030726
47595CB00003B/960